I0606239

SHIPS AHOY!
Battleships
BLASTOFF! 2 READERS
by Kaitlyn Duling
BLASTOFF! READERS, AN IMPRINT OF BELLWETHER MEDIA BY FLUTTERBEE

Blastoff! Readers are carefully developed by literacy experts to build reading stamina and move students toward fluency by combining standards-based content with developmentally appropriate text.

LEVELS

Level 1 provides the most support through repetition of high-frequency words, light text, predictable sentence patterns, and strong visual support.

Level 2 offers early readers a bit more challenge through varied sentences, increased text load, and text-supportive special features.

Level 3 advances early-fluent readers toward fluency through increased text load, less reliance on photos, advancing concepts, longer sentences, and more complex special features.

★ Blastoff! Universe

Reading Level

Grade
K

Grades
1–3

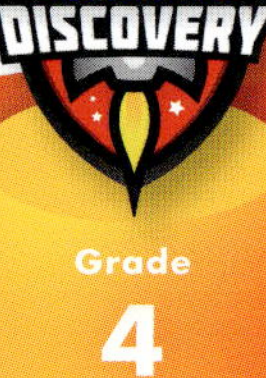

Grade
4

This edition first published in 2026 by Bellwether Media, Inc.

For information regarding permission, write to Bellwether Media, Inc., Attention: Permissions Department, 3500 American Blvd W, Suite 150, Bloomington, MN 55431.

Library of Congress Cataloging-in-Publication Data is available at www.loc.gov or upon request from the publisher.

ISBN: 9798893047981 (hardcover)
ISBN: 9798893048988 (ebook)

Editor: Kieran Downs   Designer: Jennifer Bowyer

Printed in the United States of America, North Mankato, MN.

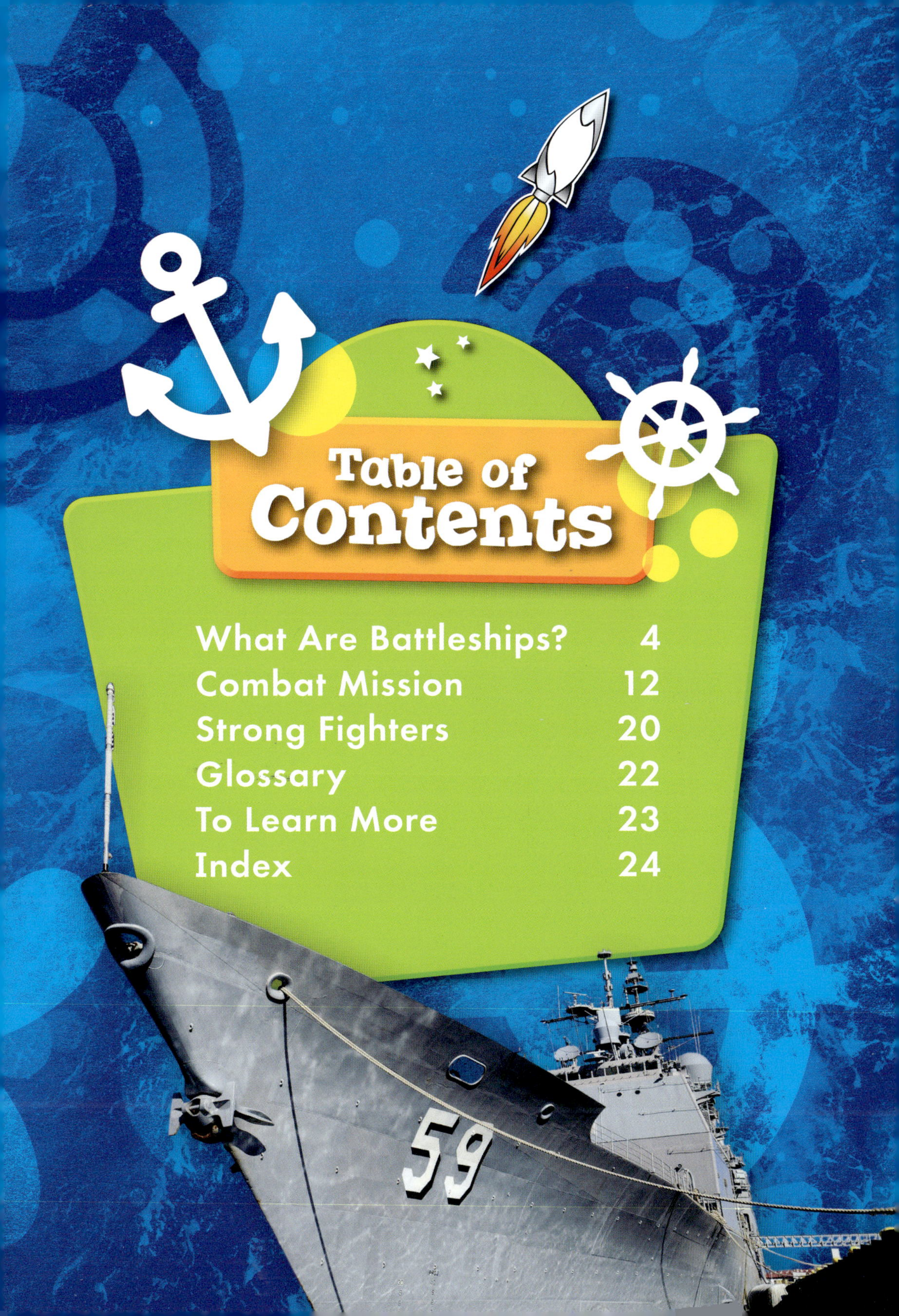

Table of Contents

What Are Battleships?

Battleships are used for **combat**. They are large and heavy.

They carry many large guns and other weapons.

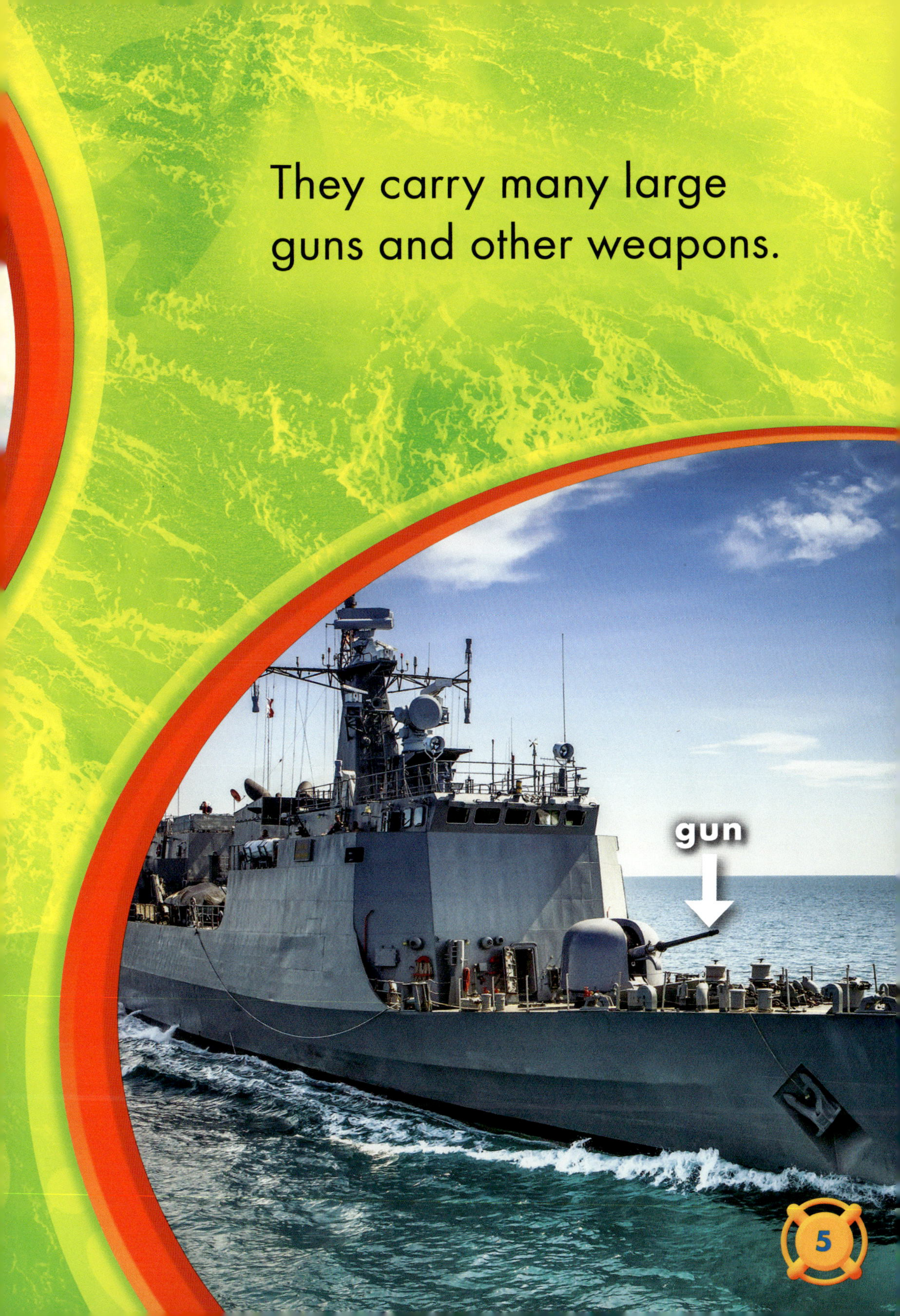

Battleships are long and narrow. A steel **hull** keeps the ship safe.

Parts of a Battleship

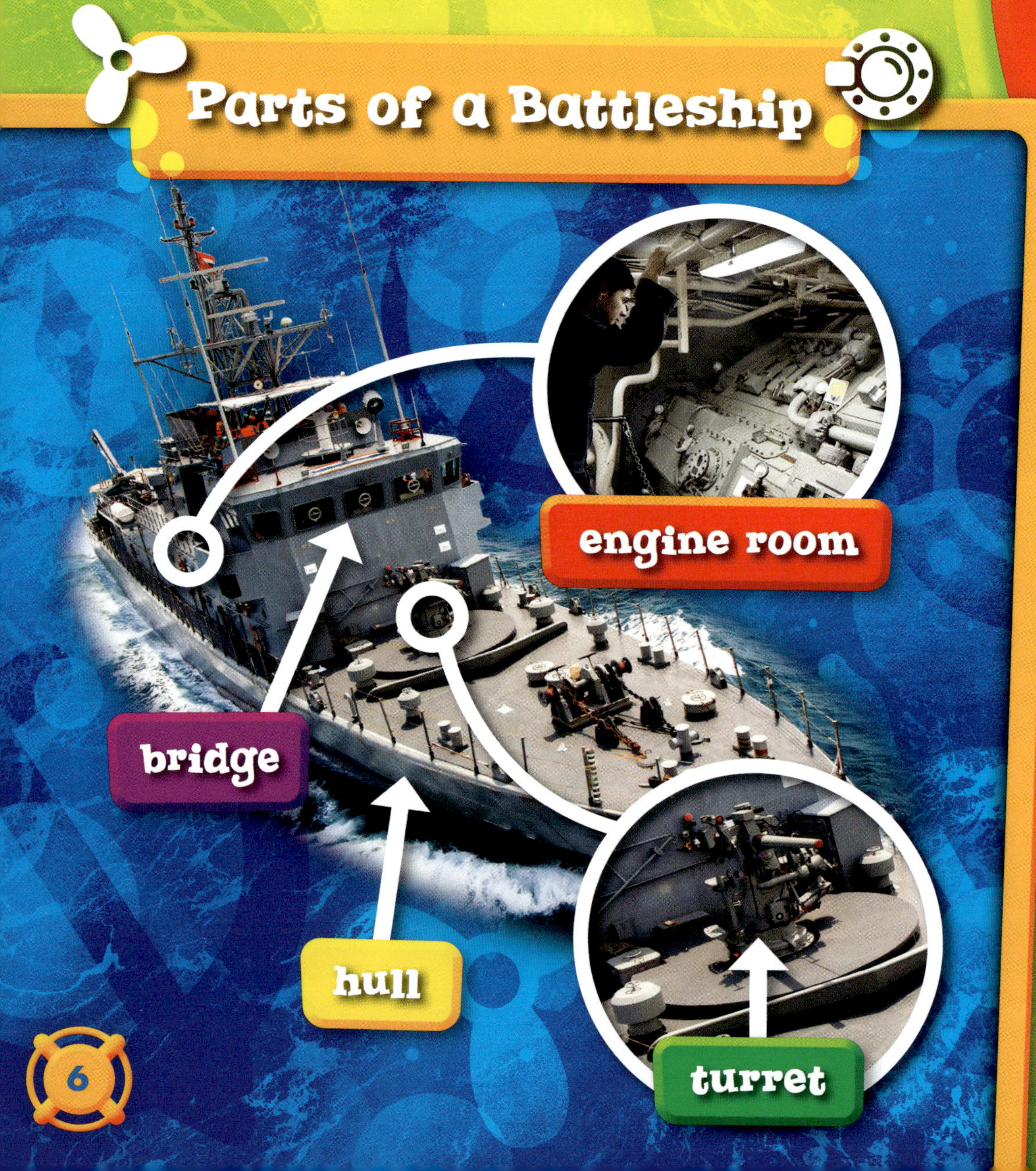

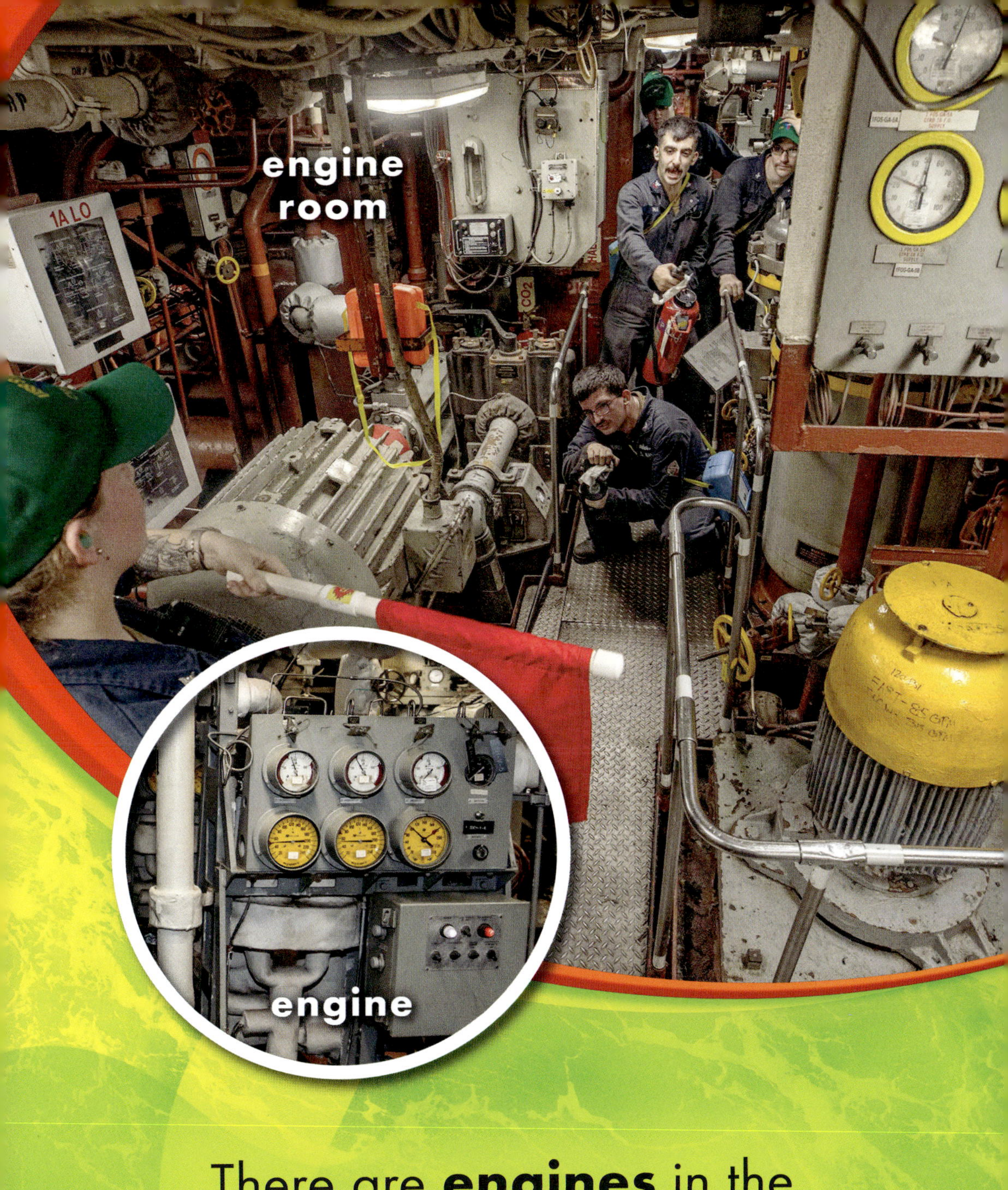

There are **engines** in the engine room. They power the ship.

Battleships are controlled from the **bridge**.

Turrets hold the ship's large guns. Each ship has many turrets.

Types of Battleships

frigate

corvette

destroyer

cruiser

Frigates are fast ships. They cross the ocean quickly. Corvettes are smaller. They travel near land.

Destroyers keep smaller ships safe. Cruisers are huge ships with many weapons.

Combat Mission

A battleship can have hundreds of crew members. They work with officers on land.

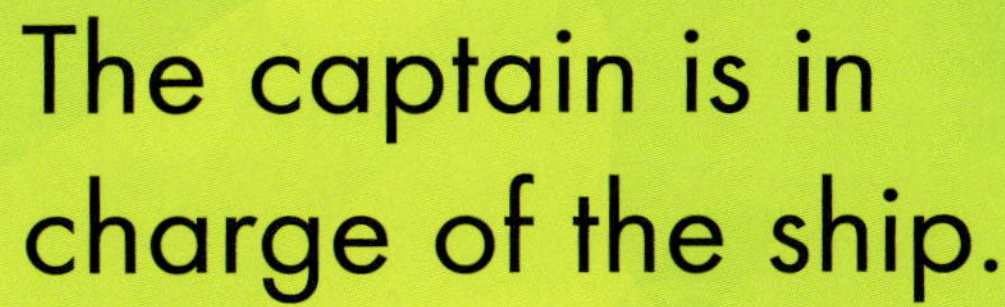

The captain is in charge of the ship.

Ship Stats

USS *Missouri* (BB-63)

Size 877 feet (270.4 meters) long; 108 feet (33 meters) wide

Type frigate

Top Speed 33 knots (38 miles or 61 kilometers per hour)

Purpose largest battleship ever built by the U.S.

Officers work on **missions**. They plan where the ship will go.

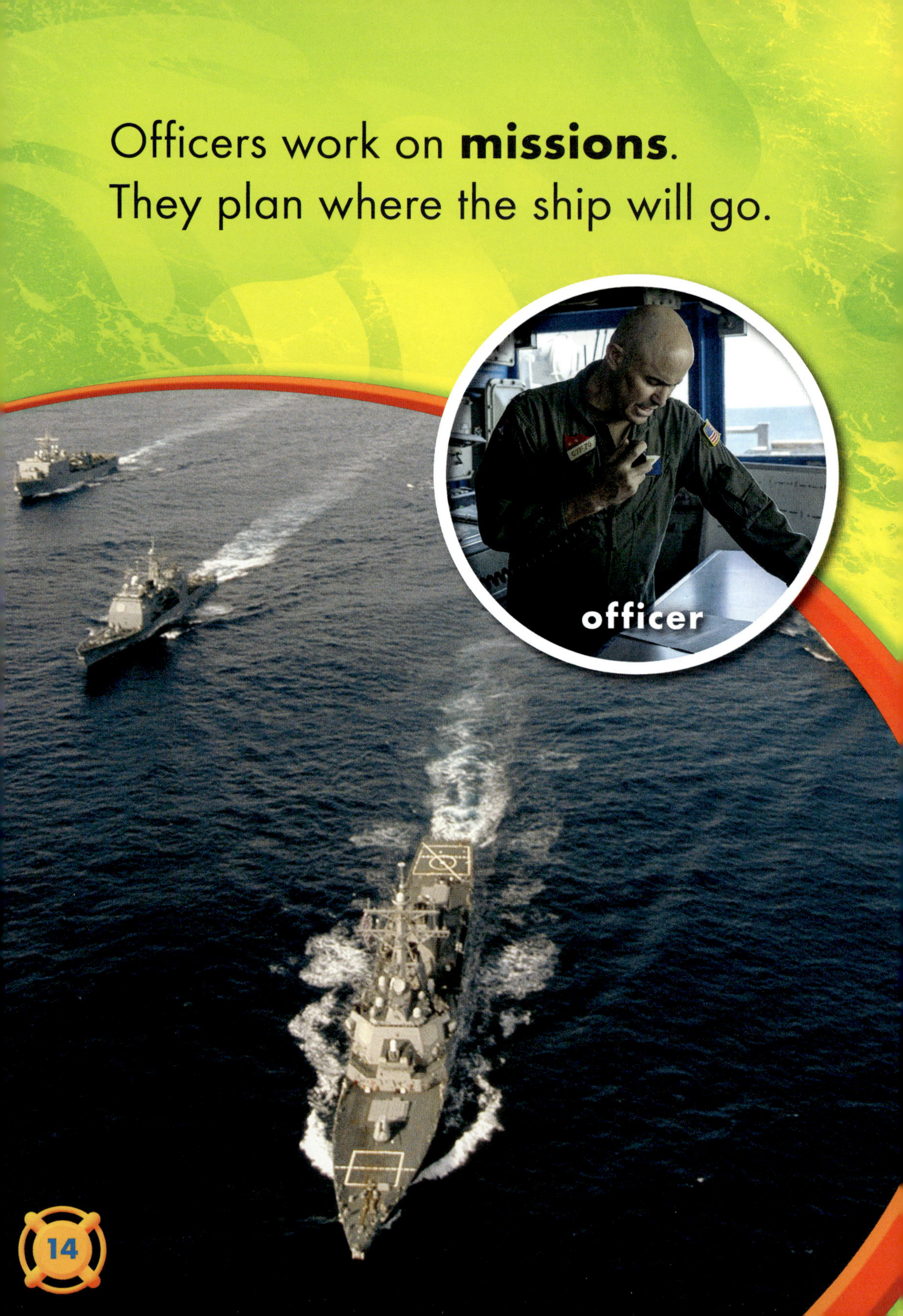

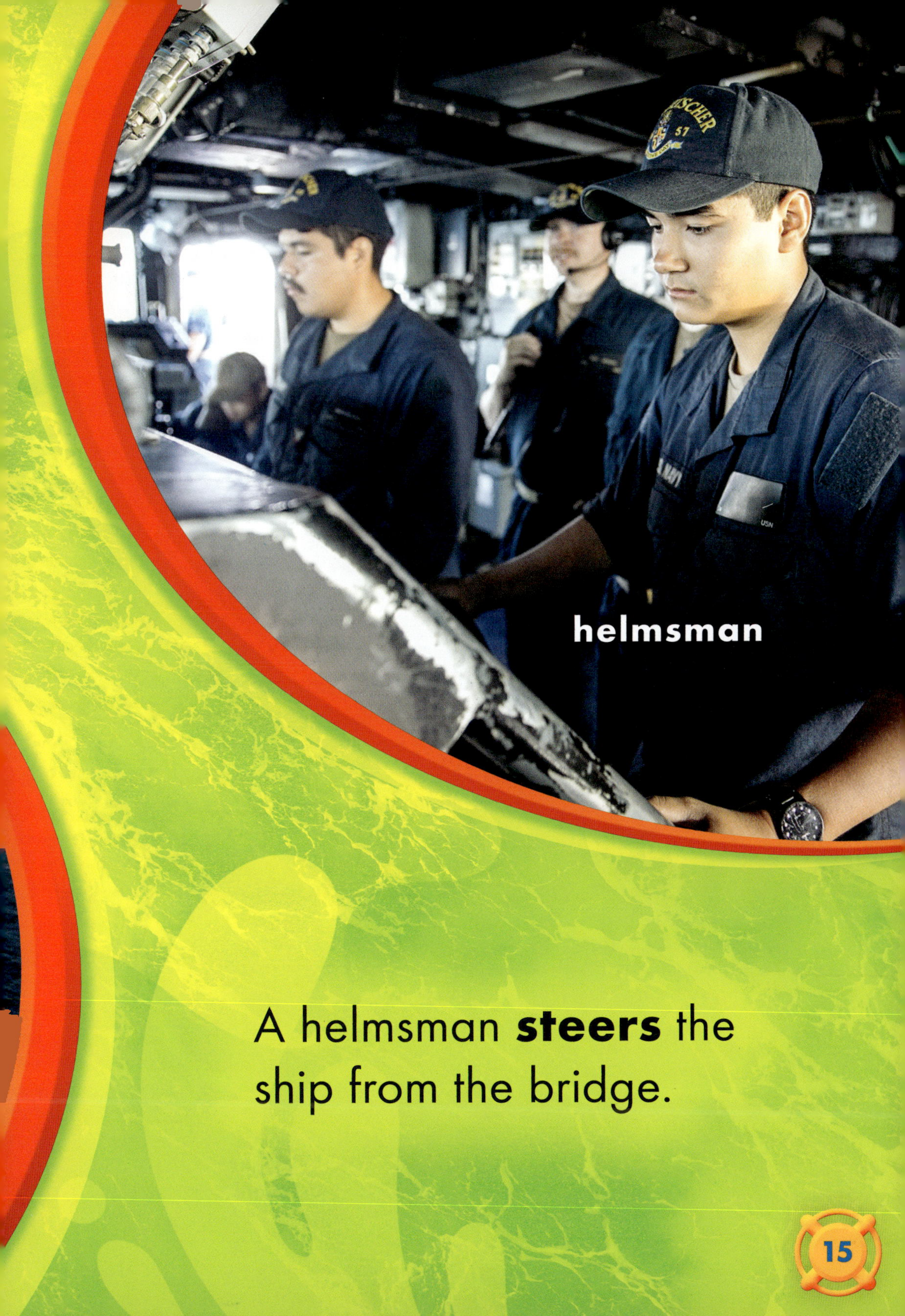

A helmsman **steers** the ship from the bridge.

Gunners work in the turrets. They load and fire the guns.

Firing from a Battleship

1 Gunners track the target.

2 The fire control system records the speed and location of the ship and its target.

3 Gunners use the information from the fire control system to aim the guns.

4 Gunners fire the guns.

Gunners use a **fire control system**. It helps them fire at the right time.

Engineers fix a battleship's engines. The engines help the ships travel all over the world.

The fastest battleships can reach speeds of around 35 **knots** (40 miles or 65 kilometers per hour).

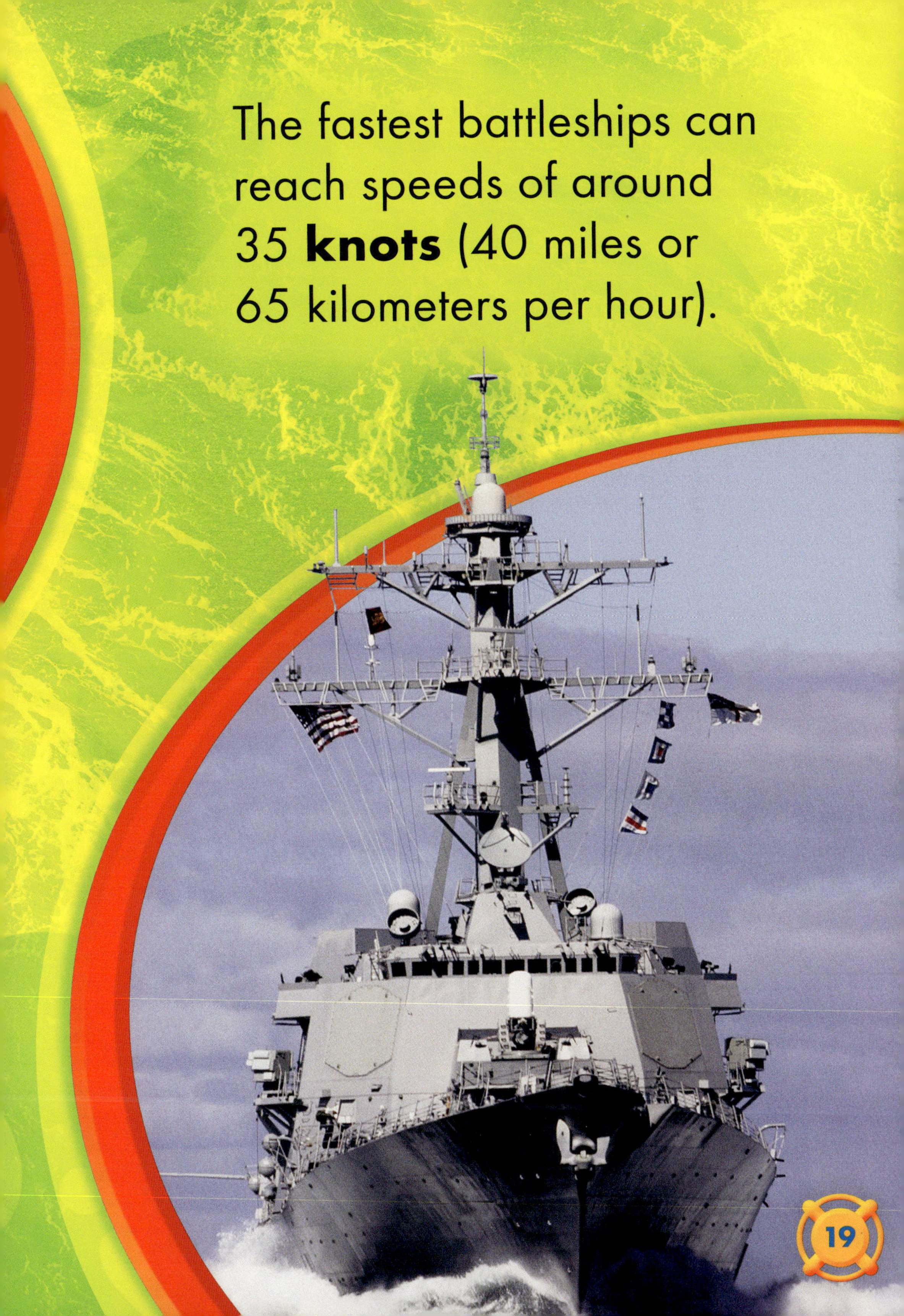

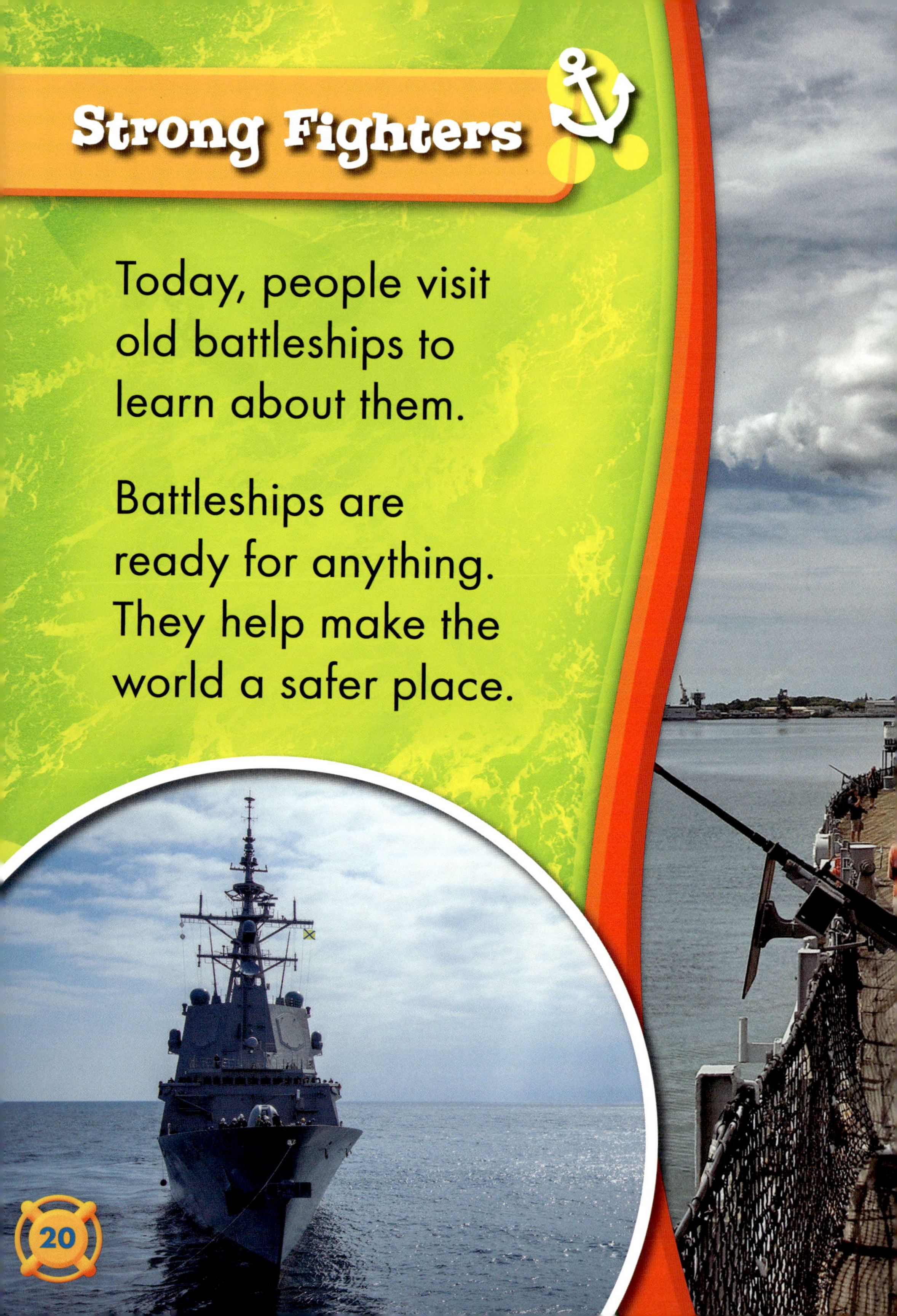

Strong Fighters

Today, people visit old battleships to learn about them.

Battleships are ready for anything. They help make the world a safer place.

U.S.S. MISSOURI BB-63

Glossary

bridge—a room where the ship is steered

combat—a fight between two people or groups

engineers—people who design engines, computers and other machines

engines—machines with moving parts that change power into motion

fire control system—a system that helps gunners aim and fire weapons at the correct time

hull—the main body of a ship

knots—units of measurement used to explain the speed of a ship

missions—tasks that a person or a group are charged with completing

steers—controls movement

turrets—small towers that hold weapons and can turn to aim

To Learn More

AT THE LIBRARY

Duling, Kaitlyn, *Aircraft Carriers*. Minneapolis, Minn.: Bellwether Media, 2026.

Koestler-Grack, Rachel A. *Curious About Destroyers*. Mankato, Minn.: Amicus Learning, 2025.

Riggs, Kate. *Battleships*. Mankato, Minn.: Creative Education and Creative Paperbacks, 2026.

ON THE WEB

FACTSURFER

Factsurfer.com gives you a safe, fun way to find more information.

1. Go to www.factsurfer.com.
2. Enter "battleships" into the search box and click 🔍.
3. Select your book cover to see a list of related content.

Index

The images in this book are reproduced through the courtesy of: FOTOGRIN, front cover, pp. 4-5; Petty Officer 2nd Class Ace-Addison TAPIT/ DVIDS, p. 3; Kanok Sulaiman, pp. 5, 6; Seaman Mark Bergado/ DVIDS, p. 6 (engine room); Kanok Sulaiman/ DVIDS, p. 6 (turret); DVIDS, pp. 6-7; Petty Officer 2nd Class Juel Foster/ DVIDS, p. 7; Petty Officer 2nd Class Peter McHaddad/ DVIDS, pp. 8, 16 (1); Michael Johansson, pp. 8-9; AlejandroCarnicero, pp. 10 (frigates), 20; The Mariner 4291, p. 10 (corvettes); Petty Officer 1st Class RJ Stratchko/ Wikipedia, p. 10 (destroyers); Gert Kromhout/ Stocktrek Images/ Getty Images, p. 10 (cruisers); Stocktrek Images/ Getty Images, pp. 10-11; Petty Officer 1st Class Jacob Allison/ DVIDS, pp. 12-13; Krumpelman Photography, p. 13; Vernon Lewis Gallery/ Stocktrek Images/ Getty Images, p. 13 (inset); Petty Officer 2nd Class Ange-Olivier Clement/ DVIDS, p. 14 (officer); Stocktrek/ Getty Images, pp. 14-15, 19; Petty Officer 1st Class William McCann/ DVIDS, p. 15; Petty Officer 1st Class Cassandra Thompson/ DVIDS, p. 16 (2); Petty Officer 2nd Class Lyle Wilkie/ DVIDS, p. 16 (3); Petty Officer 2nd Class Samantha Oblander/ DVIDS, p. 16 (4); Seaman Desmond Parks/ DVIDS, pp. 16-17; Seaman Mark Pena/ DVIDS, pp. 18-19; Bernard Spragg/ Wikipedia, pp. 20-21; travelarium.ph, p. 23.